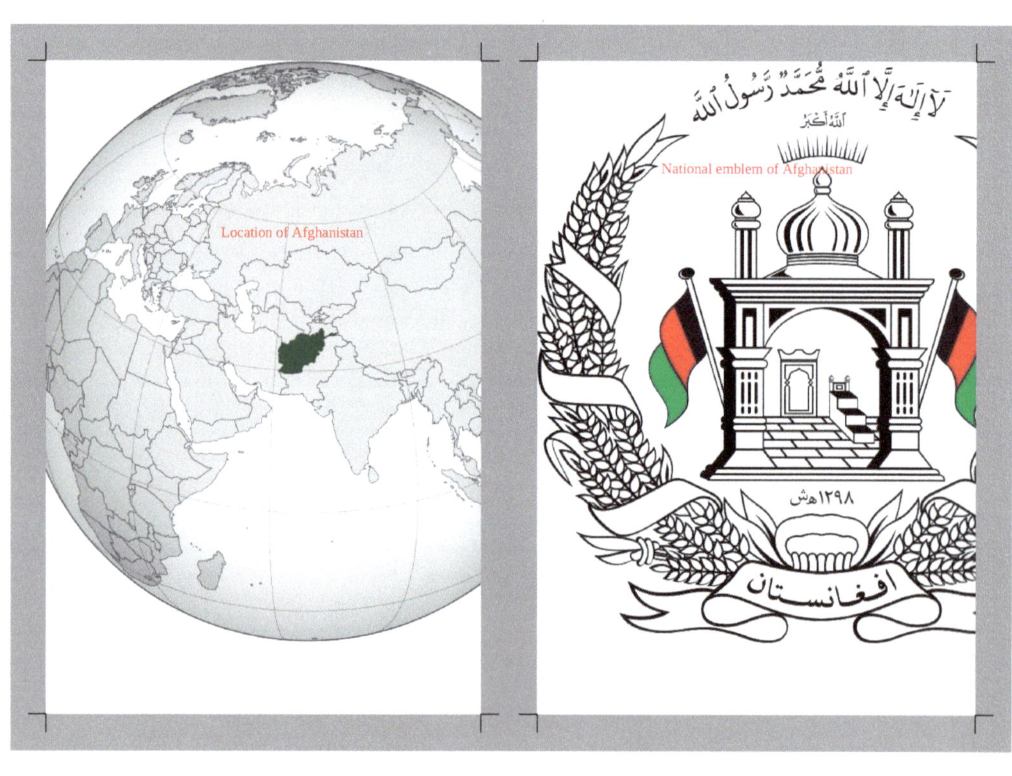

Location of Afghanistan
National emblem of Afghanistan

Citadel of Herat
Children Afghanistan Afghan Girl Boy Poverty

Boy Person Afghanistan People Happy Joy
Happiness
Soldier Uniform Army
Weapon Bullets Projectile

Face Wall Snow Steep Climbing Mountaineering
Girl Schoolgirl Learn Scholem Afghanistan Muslims

Girl Cute Afghanistan Person Alone Child
Happy
Afghanistan Kids Children Girl Boy Cute
Curious

Soldier Military Uniform Armed
Combat-Ready Battle
Daughter Child Afghanistan Father Sitting M

The taller Buddha of Bamiyan. Buddhism was widespread before the Islamic conquest of Afghanistan.

Soldiers Military Uniform Armed
Combat-Ready
Woman Old Afghanistan Person Sitting Portrait

Tradition Man Headdress Traditional Afghanistan
Man Old Afghanistan Person Thoughtful Turban

The Friday Mosque of Herat is one of the oldest mosques in Afghanistan. (March 1962 photo)
Afghanistan Man Old Weathered Staring Wary

Afghanistan School Classroom Girls Children
Children Cute Afghanistan Persons Curious Kids

Heart Soldier Military Uniform Armed Combat Ready
Afghanistan Town City People Merchants Wares

Boys Schoolboys Bamozai Afghanistan Muslims Islam
Child Dirty Poor Afghanistan Daddy Father Family

Boy Girl Children Poor House Waiting
Afghanistan
Rainbow Field Afghanistan Weather
Horizon Nature

Schoolgirls from various ethnicities in Ghazni province
Afghan boys wearing traditional headgear in Kunduz

Patrouille Army Weapons War Dangerous Afghanistan
Girl Gate Afghanistan Person Alone Child

Afghanistan Girl Burqa Ceremony Bee Keeping Women
Map Afghanistan Atlas Middle East Asia Geography

Marines Afghanistan War Soldier Taliban
Vehicle Military Tank Jeep Heavy Weather Rainy

Turban Man Praying Explaining Prophet Religions
Army Weapon Bullets Projectile War Dangerous

Boys Family Father Turban Traditional Farmers
Afghan women at a textile factory in Kabul

Afghanistan Landscape Aerial View Sky Clouds Fog
Children Sisters Traditional Garment Afghanistan

Runners Silhouette Athletes Fitness Men Militar
Shepherd Sheep Man Children Afghanistan Farm

Armed War Photographer Soldier Camera Photo
Jeep Vehicle Military Tank Heavy Weather Rainy

Children Afghanistan Curious Boys Begging Soldiers
Girl Cute Tongue Thinking Afghanistan Poverty

Woman Afghanistan Ceremony Burqa Ponder Women
Afghanistan Butterfly Delicate Special Freedom

Father Afghanistan Man Child
Mud Happy
Soldier Army Afghanistan Shooting Weapons
War

Afghanistan Landscape Sun Sunset Mountains
Afghanistan Humvee Deployment Mountains Convoy

Scout Explore Reconnoiter Sneak Up
Spotting
Refugee Young Man Portrait Male Person
Afghanistan

Rainbow Double Rainbow Tank Military Us Army
Afghanistan Houses Homes Buildings Outside

Boy Young Hope Religious Afghanistan Islamic
Children Cute Afghanistan Persons Curious Kids

Fighter Weapon Afghani Rebel War Dangerous
Afghanistan Air Base Aircraft Plane Runway Takeoff

Afghanistan Mountains Helicopter Ride Heights
Refugee Young Man Portrait Male Person Afghanistan

Army Weapons Cartridge Bullets Projectiles War
Army Patrol Afghanistan Military Vehicle Military

Military Lmtv Defense Afghanistan American Armor
Afghanistan Soldier Security Weapon Village Patrol

Horse Reiter Human Equestrian White Friends
Afghanistan Women On Internet Females Classroom

Afghanistan Remote Road Hills Mountains Rocks
Afghanistan Mountains Landscape Valley Rocks Rocky

Afghanistan A-10 Thunderbolt Ii Jet Fighter
Afghanistan Soldiers Stairs Walking Mountains

Dog Winter Snow House Afghanistan Adobe House

Infiltration Infiltrate Break In Kick Invasion
Afghanistan Mountains Sky Clouds Lake Water

Patrol Soldier Uniform Scout Explore
Reconnoiter
Afghanistan Women Man Market Goods Urban Village

Child Boy Cute Afghanistan Persons Poor Kid
Afghanistan Landscape Mountains Winter Snow Ice

Army Weapon Bullets Projectiles War Dangerous
Traction Engine Tractor Military Work Farm

Men Afghanistan Person Portrait Muslim Beard
Hindukush Afghanistan Mazar-E-Sharif Approach

Men Afghani Persons Muslim Tradition
Traditional
Man Portrait Afghanistan Village Elders
Men

Afghanistan Shooting Range Military
Afghanistan Soldier Military Uniform Armed

Army Weapon Afghani Rebel War Dangerous
Reconnoiter Scout Explore Spotting Spyglass

Afghanistan Landscape Scenic Sky Clouds Mountains
Rough Lapis Lazuli Blue Mineral Afghanistan

Afghanistan Marines Military Defensive Position Sky
Afghanistan Afghans Kandahar Kabul Herat Peo

Mantoo Food Afghanistan Cuisine Bread Ethnic Meal
Scout Defilade Reconnoiter Spot Hide Soldier Army

Afghanistan Scene War Zone Cool Army
Soldier Gun
Storm Wind Windstorm Fields Nature

Lake Mountains Sky Clouds Summer Spring
Armed Forces Soldiers Army Us Army Afghanistan War

Moped Motorcycle Handlebars Four Too Much
Kabul
Afghanistan Mountains Lake Water Grass
Moss

Afghanistan Soldier Army War Military Iraq Armed
Fortress Fort Stronghold Landscape Farmland

Army Military Vehicle Military Vehicle Afghanistan

Runner Marathon Military Afghanistan
Marines

Afghanistan Shepherd Sheep Flock Winter Cold
Soldier Skid Chain Chain Uniform Army Patrol

Afghanistan Deployment Security Farm Village
Herat Afghanistan City Urban Buildings Structures

Afghanistan Farm Woman Village Nature Farming
Afghanistan Merchant Man Village Villager Goods

Afghanistan Landscape Mountains Scenic Sky Clouds
Afghanistan Mountains Helicopter Ride Heights

Afghan Boy Afghans Afghanistan Kandahar Kabul Kid
Cirrus Clouds Sky Clouds Blue Weather Cirrus

Troopers Troops Soldiers Fields Marching Scouts
Afghanistan Landscape Winter Snow Mountains

Afghanistan Children Carrots Crop Fields Sky
Us Air Force Pallet Drops Food Afghanistan Kandahar

Runner Marathon Military Afghanistan Mari
Afghanistan Mountains Landscape Hills Nature Sky

Afghanistan Landscape Mountains Wind Farm
Man Old Afghanistan Person Thoughtful Turban

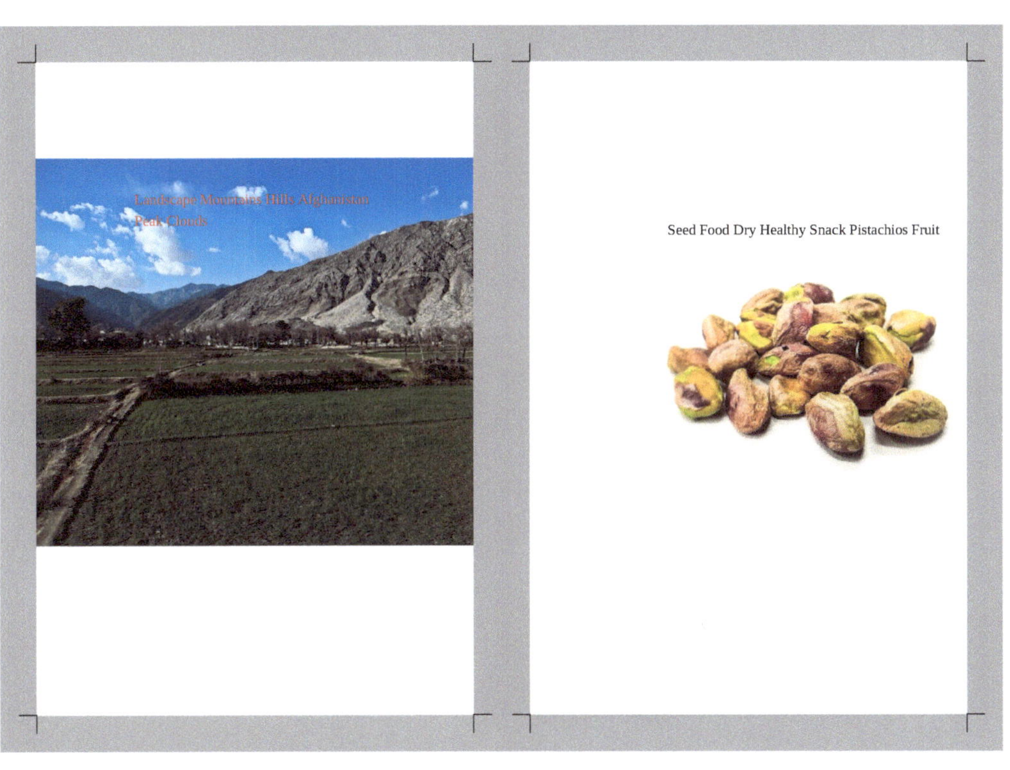

Landscape Mountains Hills Afghanistan Peak Clouds

Seed Food Dry Healthy Snack Pistachios Fruit

Winter Army Patrol Afghanistan Military Vehicle
Afghanistan Detention Center Prisoners Cells

Break Tee Coffee Tea Time Rest Enjoy Afghanistan
Soldier War Patrol Scout Explore Reconnoiter

Afghanistan Mountains Scenic Lake Water Sky
Globe Map Afghanistan Geography States Of America

Girl Afghanistan Muslims Islam Veil Joy Woman
Ride Desert Reiter Afghanistan Boy Horse

Soldier Calf Farmland Farm Cow Us Army
Dog Farm Boy Home House Poor Farmland

Kabul Children Poverty Afghanistan
Afghanistan Training Military

Jewellery Afghanistan Jewelry Ethnic Lapis Lazuli
Afghan Soldier Military Army Afghanistan War

Afghani Pulao Pilaf Afghanistan Meal Dish
Afghanistan Talks Afghan Discussion Communication

Army Isaf Afghanistan Bundeswehr Use Military
Youth Centre Girl Billiards Afghanistan Play Joy

Afghan Soldiers Military War Army
Afghanistan
Refugee Young Man Portrait Male Person
Afghanistan

Μαλακάσα Refugees Afghanist
Inspection Investigate Enter Soldier Us Army

Μαλακάσα Refugees
Afghanistan
Army Car Humvee Hummer Military
Afghanistan War

Afghanistan Sand Dust
Soldier Monument Afghanistan Kirov Memory

Saudi Arabia Bird Animal Nature Wildlife Life
Soldier Afghanistan Medal Army War Veteran
AFGHANISTAN
ELIZABETH II DEI GRATIA REGINA FID DEF
FOR OPERATIONAL SERVICE

Afghanistan Flag Land Coat Of Arms
Characters

Proof

www.ingramcontent.com/pod-product-compliance
Lightning Source LLC
Chambersburg PA
CBHW040258240726
48664CB00006B/1288